Violoncello

Arietta

40 leichte Originalstücke
für Violoncello und Klavier

40 Easy Original Pieces
for Violoncello and Piano

40 pièces faciles originales
pour violoncello et piano

leicht / easy / facile

Herausgegeben von / Edited by / Edité par
Rainer Mohrs und / and Elmar Preusser

ED 22353
ISMN 979-0-001-15857-2

www.schott-music.com

Mainz · London · Berlin · Madrid · New York · Paris · Prague · Tokyo · Toronto
© 2016 SCHOTT MUSIC GmbH & Co. KG, Mainz · Printed in Germany

Inhalt / Contents

Vorwort

Diese Sammlung leichter Stücke für Cello und Klavier ist für den Cellounterricht und das erste Vorspiel gedacht. Das Heft enthält 40 Originalstücke aus Barock, Klassik, Romantik und Moderne, die sich sehr gut für das Vorspiel an Musikschulen und als Wettbewerbsliteratur oder Prüfungsstücke eignen. Der Band versteht sich als „Fundgrube" für Lehrer, Schüler und Celloliebhaber und enthält alle wichtigen Stücke für das 1. bis 3. Unterrichtsjahr.

Die technischen Anforderungen für die linke und rechte Hand sind einfach. 25 Stücke sind in der 1. Lage spielbar, die anderen erfordern leichtes Lagenspiel in der 1.-4. Lage. Einige der in der ersten Lage spielbaren Stücke können natürlich auch mit Lagenwechseln gespielt werden, um leere Saiten zu vermeiden und zu schöneren klanglichen Ergebnissen zu kommen. Alle Vortragsstücke eignen sich in besonderer Weise für die Arbeit an Ton, Ausdruck und dynamischer Gestaltung, insbesondere die romantischen Stücke von Goltermann, Gretchaninoff, Schlemüller und Trowell. Hier finden sich auch viele Beispiele für die erste Anwendung des Vibratos. Der Titel der Sammlung („Arietta") wurde daher bewusst gewählt: Alle Stücke sind melodisch und laden dazu ein, auf dem Cello zu singen, ausdrucksvoll zu spielen und einen schönen Ton zu entwickeln.

Neben bekannten Stücken von de Fesch, Breval, Gretchaninoff oder Hindemith enthält der Band auch zahlreiche Raritäten, die zu entdecken sich lohnen: die leichte frühklassische Sonate von Cirri, Goltermanns „Trauermarsch", zwei leichte Vortragsstücke der schottischen Komponistin Marie Dare oder die romantischen Vortragsstücke von Arnold Trowell, die sehr gut auf dem Cello liegen und das Instrument mit einfachen technischen Anforderungen wunderbar zum Klingen bringen. Zum Spektrum der Celloliteratur gehören heute auch Stücke mit Pop- oder Jazzstilistik wie „Stomping Boys" von Eduard Pütz oder „Disco Hit" von Gabriel Koeppen. Hier können Themen wie ternäres Spiel (Swing), Synkopen oder akzentuierte, rhythmisch betonte Bogenführung geübt werden. Zur berühmten barocken „Arietta" von De Fesch wurde eine moderne Variante im Stil einer Popballade ergänzt, dadurch wird in Schülerkonzerten eine interessante Gegenüberstellung möglich.

Viel Spaß mit diesen schönen leichten Cellostücken!

Rainer Mohrs und Elmar Preusser

Preface

This collection of easy pieces for cello and piano is intended for cello tuition and beginners' recitals. The book contains forty original pieces from the Baroque, Classical, Romantic and modern eras suitable for music centre concerts, as repertoire for competitions or as examination pieces. This volume offers a treasure trove for teachers, pupils and amateur cellists, with plenty of useful pieces for the first three years of tuition.

Technical demands are simple for both left and right hand. Twenty-five of the pieces can be played in 1st position, with the rest requiring simple position changes in 1st to 4th position. Some of the pieces can be played either in 1st position or using position changes to avoid open strings and produce a lovelier sound. All these pieces are eminently suitable for working on tone, expression and dynamic shaping, especially the Romantic pieces by Goltermann, Gretchaninoff, Schlemüller and Trowell. Many occasions are presented for introducing the use of vibrato, too. The title of the collection, 'Arietta', was a deliberate choice: all the pieces are tuneful and invite players to make the cello sing, play with expression and develop beautiful tone.

Besides familiar classics by de Fesch, Breval, Gretchaninoff and Hindemith, the book also contains a number of rare finds well worth discovering: the easy early classical sonata by Cirri, Goltermann's 'Funeral March', two easy pieces by Scottish composer Marie Dare and Romantic pieces by Arnold Trowell that lie easily on the cello and make the instrument sound wonderful with basic technique. The modern cello repertoire also includes pieces in pop or jazz style such as 'Stomping Boys' by Eduard Pütz and 'Disco Hit' by Gabriel Koeppen. Here are practice opportunities using ternary form (swing), syncopation and accented, rhythmical bowing techniques. The well-known Baroque 'Arietta' by de Fesch is complemented by a modern version in the style of a pop ballad that presents an interesting contrast for student concert programmes.

Have fun with these lovely easy cello pieces!

Rainer Mohrs and Elmar Preusser
Translation Julia Rushworth

Arietta

Willem de Fesch
1687–1761

Larghetto e piano

aus / from: W. de Fesch, Sonate d-Moll / D minor op. 8/3, Schott CB 54

Rigaudon I

Joseph Bodin de Boismortier
ca. 1691–1755

Rigaudon II

*Rigaudon I
da Capo*

Sonata
1 Allegro

Giovanni Battista Cirri
1724–1808
B. c.: Wolfgang Birtel

aus / from: G.B. Cirri, Sonata C-Dur / C major, Schott CB 192

2 Adagio

Giovanni Battista Cirri

3 Menuetto

Giovanni Battista Cirri

14

Sonata
C-Dur / C major / Ut majeur
opus 40/1
1

Arr.: Joachim Stutschewsky
Revision: Rainer Mohrs

Jean Baptiste Bréval
1753–1823

Allegro (♩ ca. 120)

20

2 Rondo grazioso

22

Trauer
Mourning / Deuil
op. 118/2

Georg Goltermann
1824–1898

Andante

Marche funèbre
Trauermarsch / Funeral March
op. 97/2

Georg Goltermann
1824–1898

Lento ma non troppo

aus / from: G. Goltermann, Tonbilder / Musical Pictures, op. 97

Morgenspaziergang
Morning Stroll / Promenade matinale

Alexander Gretchaninoff
1864–1956

aus / from: A. Gretchaninoff, In aller Frühe / Early Morning, op. 126b, No. 1, Schott ED 2143

Heimweh
Homesickness / Nostalgie

Alexander Gretchaninoff

aus / from: A. Gretchaninoff, In aller Frühe / Early Morning, op. 126b, No. 2, Schott ED 2143

Spaßvogel
The Joker / Blagueur

Alexander Gretchaninoff

Allegretto grazioso

aus / from: A. Gretchaninoff, In aller Frühe / Early Morning, op. 126b, No. 3, Schott ED 2143

In der Dämmerung
Twilight / Au crépuscule

Alexander Gretchaninoff

aus / from: A. Gretchaninoff, In aller Frühe / Early Morning, op. 126b, No. 4, Schott ED 2143

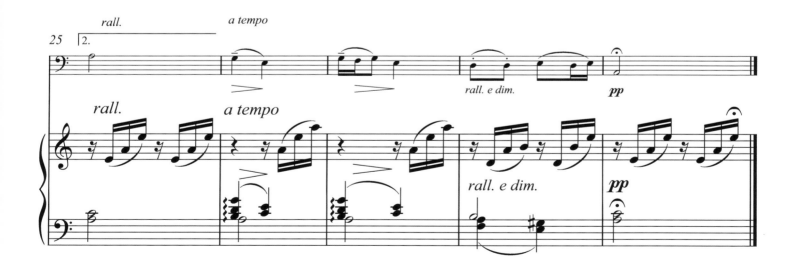

Am Winterabend
On Winter's Eve / Au soir d'hiver

Alexander Gretchaninoff

aus / from: A. Gretchaninoff, In aller Frühe / Early Morning, op. 126b, No. 6, Schott ED 2143

Burlesque

Alexander Gretchaninoff

aus / from: A. Gretchaninoff, In aller Frühe / Early Morning, op. 126b, No. 7, Schott ED 2143

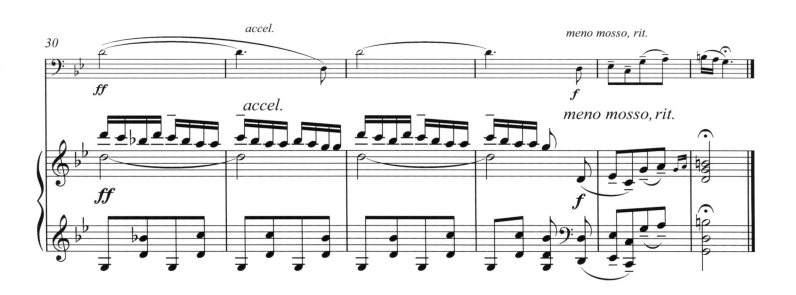

Räuber und Gendarm
Thieves and Policeman / Jeu de brigands

Alexander Gretchaninoff

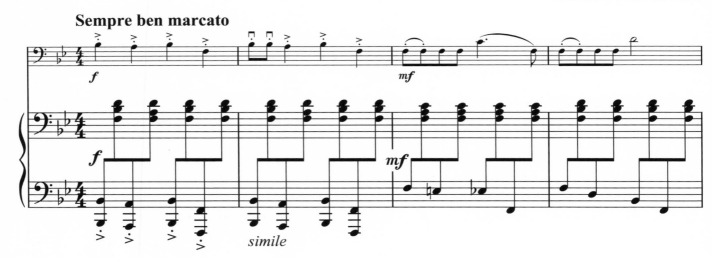

aus / from: A. Gretchaninoff, In aller Frühe / Early Morning, op. 126b, No. 9, Schott ED 2143

Walzer
Waltz / Valse

Alexander Gretchaninoff

Moderato, molto grazioso

aus / from: A. Gretchaninoff, In aller Frühe / Early Morning, op. 126b, No. 10, Schott ED 2143

Aus wendetechnischen Gründen bleibt diese Seite frei.
This page is left blank to save an unnecessary page turn.

Sechs leichte Vortragsstücke
Six Easy Concert Pieces
op. 12

1 Lied / Song

Hugo Schlemüller
1872–1918

2 Wiegenlied / Lullaby

Hugo Schlemüller

3 Scherzo

Hugo Schlemüller

Aus wendetechnischen Gründen bleibt diese Seite frei.
This page is left blank to save an unnecessary page turn.

4 Ländler / Landler

Hugo Schlemüller

5 Marsch / March

Hugo Schlemüller

Aus wendetechnischen Gründen bleibt diese Seite frei.
This page is left blank to save an unnecessary page turn.

6 Gebet / Prayer

Hugo Schlemüller

Sechs leichte Vortragsstücke
Six Easy Concert Pieces
op. 4

1 Melodie

Arnold Trowell
1887–1966

Andante

2 Idylle

Arnold Trowell

aus / from: A. Trowell, Sechs leichte Vortragsstücke / Six easy concert pieces op. 4

3 Chanson sans paroles

Arnold Trowell

4 Menuet

Arnold Trowell

TRIO

Aus wendetechnischen Gründen bleibt diese Seite frei.
This page is left blank to save an unnecessary page turn.

5 Gavotte

Arnold Trowell

6 Petite marche

Arnold Trowell

In Steady March Time (♩ = 144)

Drei leichte Stücke
Three Easy Pieces

I

Paul Hindemith
1895–1963

Mäßig schnell, munter (♩ = 92)

aus / from: P. Hindemith, Drei leichte Stücke / Three Easy Pieces, Schott ED 2771

II

Paul Hindemith

Aus wendetechnischen Gründen bleibt diese Seite frei.
This page is left blank to save an unnecessary page turn.

III

Paul Hindemith

94

Serenade

Marie Dare
1902–1976

Valse in G

Marie Dare

3 Short Stories
Prelude

Eduard Pütz
1911 – 2000

aus / from: E. Pütz, Short Stories. 10 Easy Pieces for Violoncello and Piano, Schott ED 7533

Sunny Morning

Eduard Pütz

Stomping Boys
(Blues)

Eduard Pütz

Not too fast; stomping ♩ ca. 108

Disco Hit

Gabriel Koeppen
*1958

1) „Bassdrum": Der Cellist schlägt mit der linken flachen Hand auf die Decke.
   Der Pianist klatscht oder schlägt auf einen bassig klingenden Teil des Klavieres,
   z.B. von unten gegen den Tastenkasten.
   'Bass drum': The cellist slaps the top of the cello with the flat of his left hand.
   The pianist slaps or hits a deep sounding part of the piano, e.g. the bottom side of the keyboard.

2) Cellist: Glissando in beliebiger Tonhöhe und/oder hoher Ruf auf „Huh".
   Pianist: Klatschen und/oder hoher Ruf auf „Huh".
   Cellist: glissando in any pitch and/or shouting 'hoo' in a high voice.
   Pianist: clapping and/or shouting 'hoo' in a high voice.

Percussion-Ensemble (ad lib.)

Hi-Hat/Shaker/Stimme „zick-e-zick-e"

Snare/Schlag auf Zarge/Stimme „ka"

Bass-Drum/flache Hand o. Faust auf Korpus/Stimme „dum"

In memoriam Willem de Fesch

Arietta 2015

Rainer Mohrs
*1953

111

Fine

Dal 𝄋 al Fine

Schott Music, Mainz 57 261